T0160088

ME, MYSELF
AND I

Published by OH!
20 Mortimer Street
London W1T 3JW

ISBN 978-1-80069-127-8

Compiled by: Malcolm Croft
Editorial: Lisa Dyer
Project manager: Russell Porter
Design: Luana Gobbo
Production: Freencky Portas

A CIP catalogue record for this book is available from the British Library

Printed in China

10 9 8 7 6 5

Cover illustration: Liz Ablashi/Vecteezy.com

THE LITTLE GUIDE TO
BEYONCÉ

ME, MYSELF AND I

CONTENTS

INTRODUCTION

Beyoncé Knowles-Carter is, without a doubt, the most powerful musician in the world. Her first band, Destiny's Child, has become known as more of a self-fulfilling prophecy than a pop group, a proving ground for the super-ambitious singer – she created the group when she was just nine years old! – to rise not only to a position to change the world … but to run it.

Ever since DC split in the early 2000s, Planet Earth has been on bended knee in nothing but adoration for its Queen Bey. Today, she is no longer just a singer from a girl group. She is a multi-hyphenated polymath: a businesswoman-mogul-actor-brand-mother-role model. In short, she is a titan of popular culture, an icon, a legend, a superstar. Honestly, at this point, you could throw any superlative at her and it would stick.

Despite being notoriously private about her personal life and reluctant to do interviews, when Beyoncé does speak, she is a quote machine, weighing in on everything from feminism, to fame, to food that is fried; when Beyoncé speaks, the world listens. It has no choice.

This Little Guide to Beyoncé, therefore, is not just a tiny tome of quotes—it's also Beyoncé's guide on how to live your best life, as inspirational and aspirational as any self-help book (but a lot cheaper!). "Being an icon is my dream," she once said on stage in 2011. Imagine anyone else saying that? They'd be laughed off stage in a second. And yet, for Beyoncé, that sentence feels like an understatement. For she is so much more than even an icon . . . she is the world's greatest living monomym: Beyoncé.

Don't even try imagine the world without her. It just wouldn't compare. God save the Queen.

ONE

DESTINY'S CHILD

No other woman on Earth is as beloved as Beyoncé. Her star burns as fierce as her alter-ego, Sasha.

But Beyoncé's rise to superstardom has been far from perfect, and the lessons she has learned along the way serve to teach us all . . .

She about to steam.
Stand back.

Jay-Z, about Beyoncé.

In the song 'Déjà Vu,' by Beyoncé featuring Jay-Z

Whenever I'm confused about something I ask God to reveal the answers to my questions, and he does. That's how we found our name—we opened up the Bible, and the word 'destiny' was right there.

Beyoncé, on the origins of the Destiny's Child band name.

As seen on *interviewmagazine.com*, August 2001, by Susanna Hodges and Lorraine Bracco

I now know that, yes, I am powerful. I'm more powerful than my mind can even digest and understand.

Beyoncé, discussing power.

As seen on *gq.com*, by Amy Wallace, January 10, 2013

I grew up in a very nice house in Houston, went to private school all my life, and I've never even been to the 'hood. Not that there's anything wrong with the 'hood.

Beyoncé, on her upbringing.

As seen on *interviewmagazine.com*, August 2001, by Susanna Hodges and Lorraine Bracco

I hate clubs. I hate the noise, I don't like the smell of smoke, I don't really even drink, and I'm not happy being the focus of everyone's attention. My, I sound like an old woman, don't I?

Beyoncé, discussing fame and performing.

As seen in *The Independent*, by Nick Duerden, November 20, 2004

I worked so hard during my childhood to meet this goal: By the time I was 30 years old, I could do what I want. I've reached that. I feel very fortunate to be in that position. But I've sacrificed a lot of things, and I've worked harder than probably anyone I know, at least in the music industry. So I just have to remind myself that I deserve it.

Beyoncé, discussing her work ethic.

As seen on *gq.com*, by Amy Wallace, January 10, 2013

Even now, getting covers or magazines or getting respect at labels is totally different for us, as women of color. Even though we've sold way more records than some artists and we're way more successful, they're treated like more of a priority. I hate to say that, but it's the truth.

Beyoncé, on success and race.

As seen on *interviewmagazine.com*, August 2001, by Susanna Hodges and Lorraine Bracco

I think music is something that can, and should, be used to get you into different things because eventually what goes up must come down. We're not going to be the number one group in the world forever— so you have to have something else to fall back on.

Beyoncé, on everlasting fame.

As seen on *interviewmagazine.com*, August 2001, by Susanna Hodges and Lorraine Bracco

The main thing I've learned is not to judge people. Because you don't really know how terrible it is to judge somebody until you get judged. And you don't know how terrible gossip is until the gossip is about you.

Beyoncé, on being judged.

As seen on *interviewmagazine.com*, August 2001, by Susanna Hodges and Lorraine Bracco

I look at the woman I was in my 20s and I see a young lady growing into confidence but intent on pleasing everyone around her. I now feel so much more beautiful, so much sexier, so much more interesting. And so much more powerful.

Beyoncé, discussing her recent life.

As seen in *Vogue*, by Clover Hope, August 6, 2018

When you love and accept yourself, when you know who really cares about you, and when you learn from your mistakes, then you stop caring about what people who don't know you think. Usually the person talking is just jealous or sad about themselves, and it takes going through this to realize that's how life is.

Beyoncé, on acceptance.

As seen on *interviewmagazine.com*, August 2001, by Susanna Hodges and Lorraine Bracco

One day, I counted the blemishes on my face. Got up to 35. It's so irritating to read in articles people saying, 'She thinks she's beautiful.' There's a lot of days that I wake up, and I hate how I look.

Beyoncé, on perfection.

As seen in *The Guardian*, by Jancee Dunn, June 10, 2001

"

I'm scared, be scared, allow it,
release it, move on.

"

Beyoncé, on fear of failure.

As seen on *gq.com*, by Amy Wallace, January 10, 2013

Something cracked open inside of me right after giving birth to my first daughter. From that point on, I truly understood my power, and motherhood has been my biggest inspiration.

Beyoncé, on motherhood.

As seen in *Vogue*, by Edward Enninful, November 1, 2020

I came into the music industry at 15 years old and grew up with the world watching, and I have put out projects non-stop. I released *Lemonade* during the Formation World Tour, gave birth to twins, performed at Coachella, directed *Homecoming*, went on another world tour with Jay, then *Black Is King*, all back to back. My new goal is to slow down. **"**

Beyoncé, on life after a pandemic.

As seen in *Vogue*, by Edward Enninful, November 1, 2020

During my recovery [from the birth of her twins], I gave myself self-love and self-care, and I embraced being curvier. I accepted what my body wanted to be. After six months, I started preparing for Coachella. But I was patient with myself and enjoyed my fuller curves. My kids and husband did, too.

Beyoncé, on motherhood.

As seen in *Vogue*, by Clover Hope, August 6, 2018

I come from a lineage of broken male-female relationships, abuse of power, and mistrust. Only when I saw that clearly was I able to resolve those conflicts in my own relationship [with rapper Jay-Z]. Connecting to the past and knowing our history makes us both bruised and beautiful.

Beyoncé, on marriage to Jay-Z.

As seen in *Vogue*, by Clover Hope, August 6, 2018

I approach my shows like an athlete. It's one of the reasons I connect to the Super Bowl. You know how they sit down and watch whoever they're going to play and study themselves? That's how I treat my performances. I wish I could just enjoy them, but I see the light that was late. I see, 'Oh God, that hair did not work!'

Beyoncé, on live performance.

As seen on *gq.com*, by Amy Wallace, January 10, 2013

"

I love my job, but it's more than that: I *need* it.

"

Beyoncé, on life as a superstar.

As seen on *gq.com*, by Amy Wallace, January 10, 2013

Before I gave birth to [daughter] Blue Ivy, that was the only time in my life, all throughout my life, that I was lost.

Beyoncé, on being a parent.

As seen on *gq.com*, by Amy Wallace, January 10, 2013

When I'm onstage, I don't know what the crap happens. I am gone. It's like a blackout.

Beyoncé, on performing live.

As seen on *abcnews.go.com*, January 10, 2013

The beauty of social media is it's completely democratic. Everyone has a say. Everyone's voice counts, and everyone has a chance to paint the world from their own perspective.

Beyoncé, on social media.

As seen in *Vogue*, by Clover Hope, August 6, 2018

My mother taught me the importance not just of being seen but of seeing myself.

Beyoncé, on parental advice.

As seen in *Vogue*, by Clover Hope, August 6, 2018

I will continue to explore every inch of my soul and every part of my artistry.

Beyoncé, on life as an artist.

As seen in *Vogue*, by Clover Hope, August 6, 2018

I feel like my job in the industry is to push the limits, and I have to constantly evolve.

Beyoncé, on her role within the music industry.

As seen on *billboard.com*, by Ray Rogers, November 5, 2011

I'm attracted to songs that will become a dinner conversation! With 'Single Ladies' clearly I'd just gotten married, and people want to get married every day.

Beyoncé, discussing 'Single Ladies'.

As seen on *billboard.com*, by Ray Rogers, November 5, 2011

'Crazy in Love' was another one
of those classic moments in pop
culture that none of us expected.
I asked Jay to get on the song the
night before I had to turn my album
in—thank God he did. It still
never gets old, no matter how
many times I sing it.

Beyoncé, discussing 'Crazy in Love.'

As seen on *billboard.com*, by Ray Rogers,
November 5, 2011

I can never be safe; I always try and go against the grain. As soon as I accomplish one thing, I just set a higher goal. That's how I've gotten to where I am.

Beyoncé, on career aspirations.

As seen on *billboard.com*, by Ray Rogers, November 5, 2011

We all have special numbers in
our lives, and 4 is that for me.
It's the day I was born. My mother's
birthday, and a lot of my friends'
birthdays, are on the fourth;
April 4 is my wedding date.

Beyoncé, on lucky numbers.

As seen on *newsweek.com*, by Tufayel Ahmed,
July 20, 2017

Power means happiness, power means hard work and sacrifice. To me, it's about setting a good example, and not abusing your power! You still have to have humility: I've seen how you can lead by example, and not by fear.

Beyoncé, discussing her power.

As seen on *billboard.com*, by Ray Rogers, November 5, 2011

TWO

INDEPENDENT WOMAN

In recent years, Beyoncé has extended her talents far beyond her musical capabilities by becoming an award-winning film and documentary director, producer, fashion designer, and, in her biggest challenge yet, mother.

How does she have the time to do it all? Let's find out . . .

"

I'm like a sponge and soak
everything up.

"

Beyoncé, on her inspiration.

As seen on *ew.com*, by Leah Greenblatt, May 11, 2011

At this point, I really know who I am, and don't feel like I have to put myself in a box. I'm not afraid of taking risks—no one can define me.

Beyoncé, on knowing who she is as an artist.

As seen on *ew.com*, by Leah Greenblatt, May 11, 2011

If everything was perfect, you would never learn and you would never grow. "

Beyoncé, on perfection.

As seen in the *Metro*, by Mary Olivia Hickey, September 5, 2014

I've fallen quite a few times, so I've learned how to fall. It's very rare that I'm not bruised in my life. I'm always bruised somewhere—like my legs, my hips . . .

Beyoncé, on falling while performing.

As seen in *Vogue*, by Jo Ellison, April 4, 2013

I don't like to gamble, but if there is one thing I'm willing to bet on, it is myself.

Beyoncé, on her abilities.

As seen on *abcnews.go.com*, by Lauren Sher, November 24, 2009

Whenever I've had a video that's great, I've definitely bled somewhere—the dancing, and the shoes, and the costumes—it's always a ring or something that slices me. But you've already started, so you've just gotta fight through it.

Beyoncé, on the dangers of her ambitious music videos.

As seen on *rte.ie*, April 14, 2013

I don't feel the pain on stage.
The adrenaline takes over.
But when I get off the stage?
They come off.

Beyoncé, on high heels.

As seen in *Vogue*, by Jo Ellison, April 4, 2013

Why do you have to choose what type of woman you are? Why do you have to label yourself anything? I'm just a woman and I love being a woman. If you're attractive then you can't be sexy, and you can't be intelligent? What is all of that?

Beyoncé, on the power of women.

As seen in *The Independent*, by Beckie Smith, April 12, 2013

I am a modern-day feminist. I do believe in equality, and that we have a way to go and it's something that's pushed aside and something that we have been conditioned to accept. But I'm happily married. I love my husband. "

Beyoncé, on feminism.

As seen on *nme.com*, by Jenny Stevens, April 4, 2013

I feel like Mrs. Carter is who I am,
but I am more bold and more
fearless than I've ever been.

Beyoncé, on marriage to Jay-Z.

As seen in *Rolling Stone*, by RJ Cubarrubia,
April 3, 2013

On stage, I can say anything,
I can be goofy, sexy, anything
that I feel.

Beyoncé, on her live performances.

As seen in *Vogue*, by Jo Ellison, April 4, 2013

After the Super Bowl, I took a week and I ate everything I wanted to. From doughnuts to cheeseburgers to fried fish—I even had fried alligator. Anything fried.

Beyoncé, on her love of fried food.

As seen in the *Evening Standard*, by Unity Blatt, April 9, 2013

As long as I could sing, I would be happy. It just feels good to my body.

Beyoncé, on her love of singing.

As seen in *Vogue*, by Jo Ellison, April 4, 2013

Everyone in my life serves a different purpose and has a different ear, and a different type of advice. But I have to make the decisions.

Beyoncé, on her entourage.

As seen on *cleopatrasworldwide.com*, August 27, 2018

I'm not just self-critical. I'm critical.
I'm not so critical that I don't
understand what's great and what's
not, but I do push people. I push
them and I push myself. It's just who
I am. I was that way when I was
nine years old. And no one taught
me that, it's just who I was.

Beyoncé, on self-criticism.

As seen in *Vogue*, by Jo Ellison, April 4, 2013

I definitely want my daughter to have goals and drive and passion —but it has to be a balance. Whatever makes her happy, I'm there.

Beyoncé, discussing her daughter.

As seen on *capitalfm.com*, April 3, 2013

We all have our imperfections.
But I'm human, and you know, it's
important to concentrate on other
qualities besides outer beauty.

Beyoncé, on her imperfections.

As seen in the *Metro*, by Mary Olivia Hickey,
September 5, 2014

We were really sheltered. After the show we would get on the tour bus and read the Bible.

Beyoncé, discussing her upbringing.

As seen in *OK!* magazine, December 4, 2018

There are a lot of things I never did [while touring] because I believe in watching those true Hollywood stories and I see how easy it is to lose track of your life. Think about Marilyn Monroe.

Beyoncé, on the perils of fame.

As seen in *Elle*, by Will Blythe, December 4, 2008

I grew up upper-class. Private school. My dad had a Jaguar. We're African-American and we work together as a family, so people assume we're like the Jacksons. But I didn't have parents using me to get out of a bad situation.

Beyoncé, on her upbringing.

As seen in *Elle*, by Will Blythe, December 4, 2008

I taught my girls to pick up their own suitcases. Pretty is as pretty does. Like my mother said, 'You got to be cute on the inside.'

Tina Knowles, on her children's upbringing.

As seen in *Elle*, by Will Blythe, December 4, 2008

The trick to love is to find somebody who makes you a better person. You are who you're around. And if I don't want to be like you, I don't want to be around you.

Beyoncé, on hanger-ons and love.

As seen in *Elle*, by Will Blythe, December 4, 2008

I'm not bossy. I'm the boss.

Beyoncé, on who's the boss (for a female empowerment campaign).

As seen in *Rolling Stone*, by Ryan Reed, March 10, 2014

I put a lot of thought into how I wanted to unveil my pregnancy. It was important to me that I was able to do it myself. I decided to say nothing and proudly show my baby bump. I felt it was more powerful to see the love and enthusiasm as opposed to saying anything.

Beyoncé, on being pregnant with Blue Ivy.

As seen in *Harper's Bazaar*, by Elisa Lipsky-Karasz, October 11, 2011

I have been pregnant through every major event I've done, from the Billboard Awards to Glastonbury.

Beyoncé, on pregnancy.

As seen in *Harper's Bazaar*, by Elisa Lipsky-Karasz, October 11, 2011

If you want to see the Third Ward Texas come out in me, disrespect my sister, and I will go completely crazy on you.

Beyoncé, talking about her sister, Solange Knowles.

As seen in *Harper's Bazaar*, by Elisa Lipsky-Karasz, October 11, 2011

It was important to me that I gave myself time to focus on becoming the woman I want to be, building my empire, my relationship, and my self-worth, before I became a mother.

Beyoncé, on her empire.

As seen in *The Hollywood Reporter*, by Lyndsay Powers, October 11, 2011

The best thing about marriage is the amount of growth you have because you can no longer hide from your fears and insecurities. There's someone right there calling you out on your flaws and building you up when you need the support. If you are with the right person, it brings out the best version of you.

Beyoncé, on marriage.

As seen in *Harper's Bazaar*, by Elisa Lipsky-Karasz, October 11, 2011

I am finally at the stage in my life where I am not so concerned with other people's opinions about my life decisions. It is so liberating to really know what I want, what truly makes me happy, what I will not tolerate. I have learned that it is no one else's job to take care of me but me.

Beyoncé, on self-reflection.

As seen in *Harper's Bazaar*, by Elisa Lipsky-Karasz, October 11, 2011

I'm thankful for my life, I'm thankful for my health and my family, and for music, and for having the best job in the world.

Beyoncé, on being thankful.

As seen on *abcnews.go.com*, by Lauren Sher, November 24, 2009

When I work, I don't eat. I don't use the restroom. And I think my team is just as crazy as I am because they are right there with me pushing it and pushing themselves.

Beyoncé, on her intense work ethic.

As seen on *abcnews.go.com*, by Lauren Sher, November 24, 2009

People don't know that these songs
meant more than just the songs
that are catchy. It's my life.

Beyoncé, on her music.

As seen on *abcnews.go.com*, by Lauren Sher,
November 24, 2009

My whole objective here is for people to see what they don't get to see. Just give me my band, give me a stage, some cool smoke and lights, and you see the sweat, you see the pain, you see the love, you see the soul, and it's about music.

Beyoncé, on performing live.

As seen on *abcnews.go.com*, by Lauren Sher, November 24, 2009

There's an actual story behind all of my songs and why I wrote those songs. A lot of the people in the audience would know 'Crazy in Love,' but would not particularly know this is when I met my first love ... my husband.

Beyoncé, on the meaning of her songs.

As seen on *abcnews.go.com*, by Lauren Sher, November 24, 2009

I always will believe in the strength we have as women. And there are certain things you should not put up with and you have the choice to set the standards.

Beyoncé, on feminism.

As seen on *abcnews.go.com*, by Lauren Sher, November 24, 2009

There would definitely not be a
Beyoncé without Destiny's Child.
I love my girls.

Beyoncé, on Destiny's Child.

As seen on *abcnews.go.com*, by Lauren Sher,
November 24, 2009

I don't need Sasha Fierce so much anymore because these days I know who I am.

Beyoncé, on her alter-ego, Sasha Fierce.

As seen in *Allure*, Michael Thompson, January 18, 2010

I don't like too much structure. I like to be free. I'm not alive unless I am creating something. I'm not happy if I'm not creating, if I'm not dreaming, if I'm not creating a dream and making it into something real. I'm not happy if I'm not improving, evolving, moving forward, inspiring, teaching, and learning.

Beyoncé, on art as creation.

As seen in *Vogue*, by Clover Hope, August 6, 2018

For me, balance is always really hard to find. I love so many different things, and to have the discipline to turn certain things away and focus on one thing at a time so that I can give it 100 percent is really hard.

Beyoncé, on focus.

As seen in *Pride* magazine, August 17, 2010

I think a beautiful woman is someone who is confident but not competitive with other women —someone who is warm to everyone. Because my mother told me ever since I can remember that beauty is from within, that looks will fade, I have always been aware that you have to have something deeper to be really beautiful.

Beyoncé, on defining beauty.

As seen in *The Independent*, by Beckie Smith, April 12, 2013

I think we learn a lot from our female friends—female friendship is very, very important. It's good to support each other and I do try to put that message in my music.

Beyoncé, on female friendships.

As seen in the *Daily Mail*, by Jane Gordon, August 15, 2010

I'm never satisfied. I'm sure
sometimes it's not easy working
for me. I've never met anyone
that works harder than me in
my industry.

Beyoncé, on her work ethic.

As seen in *Forbes*, by Lacey Rose, June 4, 2009

I've worked too hard and sacrificed too much to do something silly that would mess up the brand I've created all of these years.

Beyoncé, on sacrifice and her brand.

As seen in *The Guardian*, by Caspar Llewellyn Smith, November 29, 2009

Just because you're a celebrity,
people feel like they have
to know everything about you.
I disagree.

Beyoncé, on celebrity.

As seen in *Forbes*, by Lacey Rose, June 4, 2009

Right now, the tabloids are saying I'm pregnant, and they're naming the baby. It's hilarious. I don't know when I'll want to get married. I never pictured myself as a bride, but after my sister's wedding, I did start thinking about what kind of wedding I'd want. I don't think I want a big one.

Beyoncé, on fame and children.

As seen in *Cosmopolitan*, by Lesley Rotchford, November 1, 2006

We decide everything together.
My word is my word. What Jay
and I have is real. It's not about
interviews or getting the right
photo op. It's real.

Beyoncé, on marriage.

As seen in *Essence*, December 16, 2009

QUEEN BEY

Beyoncé's famed for her philanthropy and her aspirational messages of hope to those who have little.

Along with her powerful lyrics of determination and courage, Beyoncé's a walking, talking positivity icon, with more than enough sage soundbites to shake a booty at . . .

When I was little, my head was smaller and I looked like I had big Dumbo ears. I still do not wear my ears out, and that's why I wear big earrings, because they camouflage your ears.

Beyoncé, on her appearance.

As seen in *Rolling Stone*, by Jancee Dunn, May 24, 2001

My life is perfect now. People want to read about us and the old members, and how we didn't get along. Who cares? It's done. We do get along, we do love each other and support each other.

Beyoncé, on Destiny's Child.

As seen in *Rolling Stone*, by Jancee Dunn, May 24, 2001

I've spent a lot of time focusing on building my legacy and representing my culture the best way I know how. Now, I've decided to give myself permission to focus on my joy.

Beyoncé, on her legacy.

As seen in the *Evening Standard*, by Lizzie Edmonds, October 31, 2020

My best advice is to love them harder than ever. I let my children know that they are never too young to contribute to changing the world. I never underestimate their thoughts and feelings.

Beyoncé, on parenting in a pandemic.

As seen in *Vogue*, by Edward Enninful, November 1, 2020

It took Destiny's Child nine years
to get on MTV.

Beyoncé, on early fame.

As seen in *The Guardian*, by Lucy O'Brien,
April 24, 2013

People have tried to get us into bathing suits, but there's a line we draw. We wear nothin' with our butt cheeks out, our boobs out. We like sexy clothes, but still classy. Not so people can say, 'How can they wear that and be a Christian?'

Beyoncé, on staying classy.

As seen in *The Guardian*, by Lucy O'Brien, April 24, 2013

I'd like to be like Barbra Streisand, doing concerts whenever I want. Sometimes I think that after a while I'm going to move away and sing in a bar somewhere, because I am a little afraid of being *too* famous.

Beyoncé, on too much fame.

As seen on *richardbenson.com*, 2003

If you see me on TV, I'm not a humble, shy person, but it's a transformation into that. It's a job. In real life I'm not like that. **"**

Beyoncé, on being a pop star.

As seen in *Rolling Stone*, by Touré, March 4, 2004

I always held back in Destiny's Child, because I was comfortable in a group and felt that I didn't have to do anything 100 percent, because there were other people onstage with me.

Beyoncé, on Destiny's Child.

As seen in *Vanity Fair*, by Lisa Robinson, November 2005

I never really told anybody who I really am. I battle with it, because at the end of the day, my life and my family are so much more important than any of this.

Beyoncé, on fame.

As seen in *The Gentlewoman*, by Paul Flynn, July 2013

I need to be able to go places and have normal conversations with people. You don't have to alienate yourself from the world.

Beyoncé, on fame.

As seen in *The Gentlewoman*, by Paul Flynn, July 2013

I think about Madonna and how she started the label and developed other artists. There are not enough of those women.

Beyoncé, on industry influences.

As seen in *The Gentlewoman*, by Paul Flynn, July 2013

In the end I became a mother, which is the biggest accomplishment of my life.

Beyoncé, on motherhood.

As seen in *The Gentlewoman*, by Paul Flynn, July 2013

The woman who gave us our record deal, I met her when I was ten, when Destiny's Child auditioned for Columbia Records.

Beyoncé, on her early career.

As seen in *The Gentlewoman*, by Paul Flynn, July 2013

In this industry, the biggest mistake
is not being in your right mind,
and then not making the right
judgment.

Beyoncé, on the music industry.

As seen in *The Gentlewoman*, by Paul Flynn, July 2013

I feel like my father taught me so much, and he prepared me for this. I always ran my stuff, since we were 15 years old. Now I'm controlling my content, controlling my brand, and archiving it for my daughter and making sure she has it and she respects it.

Beyoncé, on her father, Mathew Knowles.

As seen in *The Gentlewoman*, by Paul Flynn, July 2013

You see Puffy and you see my husband and you see these male artists that become moguls, and the female artists might become legends, but there's not enough of us that become moguls.

Beyoncé, on female businesswomen.

As seen in *The Gentlewoman*, by Paul Flynn, July 2013

People don't understand the amount of studying and research that goes into greatness. But I absolutely understand it.

Beyoncé, on greatness.

As seen in *The Gentlewoman*, by Paul Flynn, July 2013

I don't really have to do anything that I don't want to do anymore. And that feels damn good. **"**

Beyoncé, on success.

As seen in *The Gentlewoman*, by Paul Flynn, July 2013

BEYONCÉ

Light some candles, have a good
meal, and watch an old movie.
I don't cook much, but I'm good
at spaghetti and sandwiches.
I know they're easy, but they're
my specialty.

Beyoncé, on her perfect night in.

As seen in *Cosmopolitan*, by Lesley Rotchford,
November 1, 2006

You definitely feed off the people around you, and your man is one of the people you talk to the most. So you kind of help each other and keep each other strong. It's important.

Beyoncé, on what makes marriage work.

As seen in *Cosmopolitan*, by Lesley Rotchford, November 1, 2006

My mother was such a great mother and is still such a big part of my life. I want my kids to feel that way about me. I want to be in their lives. I don't want to be away a lot, so I'm sure I'll slow down. But there are so many amazing people who do both.

Beyoncé, on her mother, Tina Knowles.

As seen in *Cosmopolitan*, by Lesley Rotchford, November 1, 2006

I began to search for deeper meaning when life began to teach me lessons I didn't know I needed. Success looks different to me now. I learned that all pain and loss is in fact a gift. Having miscarriages taught me that I had to mother myself before I could be a mother to someone else.

Beyoncé, on mothering.

As seen in *Elle*, September 12, 2019

I took a risk with acting. It was scary because it was different for me. You just always have to take risks. I always go with my gut, and it's always right. People are scared to do that.

Beyoncé, on acting.

As seen in *Cosmopolitan*, by Lesley Rotchford, November 1, 2006

In my 'Crazy in Love' video, I was dancing so hard that my whole dress completely fell off in front of all these men.

Beyoncé, on 'Crazy in Love.'

As seen in *Cosmopolitan*, by Lesley Rotchford, November 1, 2006

It gets easier to be confident about my body as I get older. I realize who I am, and I deal with it. I'm still kind of embarrassed that I wrote 'Bootylicious.' I had gained a little weight, and I was making fun of it. It's a silly song, but it's nice because it's made curvy women feel sexy.

Beyoncé, on her voluptuousness.

As seen in *Cosmopolitan*, by Lesley Rotchford, November 1, 2006

If I have a day off, sometimes I'll stay in bed all day and watch TV and eat whatever I want. I'll eat cereal and Oreos and change channels every three minutes.

Beyoncé, on taking a day off.

As seen in *Cosmopolitan*, by Lesley Rotchford, November 1, 2006

"
I needed a break. I needed my dad.
I had to let go.
"

Beyoncé, on firing her manager, her father.

As seen in the documentary *Beyoncé: Life Is But a Dream*,
HBO, 2013

I love my husband, but it is nothing like a conversation with a woman that understands you. I grow so much from those conversations.

Beyoncé, on womanhood.

As seen in *Elle*, by Natasha Bird, March 31, 2016

It's difficult being a woman. It's so much pressure, and we need that support sometimes. We're all going through our problems, but we all have the same insecurities and we all have the same abilities and we all need each other.

Beyoncé, on being a woman.

As seen in the *Metro*, by Mary Olivia Hickey, September 5, 2014

It's every woman's dream to feel this way about someone. **"**

Beyoncé, on her husband, Jay-Z.

As seen in the documentary Beyoncé: Life Is But a Dream, HBO, 2013

I'm like most women—very generous, and I'll compromise. I used to be afraid of people thinking I was difficult or too critical, and you know, I don't really care about that anymore. Be your own advocate, no matter who thinks you're 'difficult.'

Beyoncé, on being considered a diva.

As seen in the documentary Beyoncé: Life Is But a Dream, HBO, 2013

People call me a diva because I'm the lead singer, so they think I'm a diva and go around kicking people out of the group.

Beyoncé, on being labeled a diva.

As seen on *nme.com*, by Tom Skinner, December 10, 2019

I was always really quiet and shy, but I felt at home on stage. I felt I could step out of myself. Because I'm a very private person and I am not the type of personality that enjoys being looked at all the time. At a party I'm the one hanging back, observing other people. But on stage I felt at home.

Beyoncé, on her love of the stage.

As seen in the *New Zealand Herald*, by Tom Horan, December 20, 2008

That is my alter-ego and now she has a last name. I have someone else that takes over when it's time for me to work and when I'm on stage, this alter-ego that I've created that kind of protects me and who I really am.

Beyoncé, on her alter-ego, Sasha Fierce.

As seen in *The Guardian*, Paul, MacInnes, October 24, 2008

It can be hard not to lose the plot.
When magazines retouch you to
make you look perfect, and you
start to believe that you really look
like that. And you can be rude to
people and no one says anything
'cos they want their jobs. You can
very easily lose perspective.

Beyoncé, on beauty and the media.

As seen in the *New Zealand Herald*, by Tom Horan,
December 20, 2008

I over-analyze everything. I want to be the best at everything, and maybe that's just me being an over-achiever. I just wish I was better at everything.

Beyoncé, on her flaws.

As seen in the *New Zealand Herald*, by Tom Horan, December 20, 2008

The girls from Destiny's Child, we would put our hair on the ironing board, and iron it, which is so crazy! My mom who used to own a hair salon was like, 'We have to get you out of your own hair, because you are destroying it!'

Beyoncé, on her beauty treatments.

As seen in *Allure*, by Kate Sullivan, March 9, 2010

I don't want to get addicted to fame. Then when I'm no longer famous, I won't know what to do, and I'll just seem desperate and lose my mind.

Beyoncé, on fame.

As seen in *Rolling Stone*, by Touré, March 4, 2004

When you work so much like we did, it's just too much. You lose touch with who you are.

Beyoncé, on early fame.

As seen in *Rolling Stone*, by Touré, March 4, 2004

My mother instilled in me the idea that creativity starts with taking a leap of faith—telling your fears they are not allowed where you are headed.

Beyoncé, on her mother, Tina Knowles.

As seen in *Elle*, December 9, 2019

In relationships, I think a lot like a guy. If I do something wrong, I don't get emotional. I think about it, and I change it, and fix it. I've always been very logical.

Beyoncé, on relationships.

As seen in *Rolling Stone*, by Touré, March 4, 2004

I remember walking out and I was
scared, but when the music started,
I don't know what happened.
I just ... changed.

Beyoncé, on becoming a singer.

As seen in *Rolling Stone*, by Touré, March 4, 2004

I used to like when people made me mad. I'm like, 'Please piss me off before the performance.' I used to use everything.

Beyoncé, on performing live.

As seen in *Rolling Stone*, by Touré, March 4, 2004

You know, equality is a myth, and for some reason, everyone accepts the fact that women don't make as much money as men do. I don't understand that. Why do we have to take a back seat?

Beyoncé, on equality.

As seen in *The Independent*, by Aisha Mirza, January 18, 2013

I truly believe that women should be financially independent from their men. And let's face it, money gives men the power to run the show. It gives men the power to define value. They define what's sexy. And men define what's feminine. It's ridiculous.

Beyoncé, on equality.

As seen in *The Independent*, by Aisha Mirza, January 18, 2013

I would not be the woman I am if I did not go home to that man. It just gives me such a foundation. We were friends first for a year and a half before we went on any date—on the phone for a year and a half.

Beyoncé, on her husband, Jay-Z.

As seen in *People*, February 15, 2013

What does fear taste like?
Success. I have accomplished
nothing without a little taste
of fear in my mouth.

Beyoncé, on fear.

As seen in *Grazia*, by Emma Spedding, October 21, 2015

The sexiest thing about a man is someone being very smart and confident. And someone who doesn't try—just is cool and naturally sexy.

Beyoncé, on men.

As seen on *complex.com*, April 2003

I feel like if men really like you, then they'll approach you. I don't feel like you should go after a man.

Beyoncé, on men.

As seen on *complex.com*, April 2003

MRS. CARTER

Beyoncé's betrothed, the legendary rapper, Jay-Z, a.k.a. Shawn Carter, may not be the perfect husband, but their decade-long marriage has cemented the couple, along with their famous children, as America's next superstar dynasty.

But being a celebrated wife and mother isn't always easy . . .

I don't feel like I have to please anyone. I feel free. I feel like I'm an adult. I'm grown. I can do what I want. I can say what I want. I can retire if I want. That's why I've worked hard.

Beyoncé, on the value of hard work.

As seen in *Time*, Jessie Van Amburg, September 2, 2016

Over time, I have learned to focus on the things I want to focus on in the time frame that I set. I no longer have to work based on someone else's expectations or pressure. I put enough pressure on myself!

Beyoncé, on personal expectations.

As seen on *billboard.com*, by Adelle Platon, March 3, 2016

I felt like I had been so commercially successful, but that wasn't enough. There's something really stressful about having to keep up with that. You can't express yourself. You can't grow. It is the battle of my life. So I set a goal. And my goal was independence.

Beyoncé, on independence.

As seen in *The New Republic*, by Noreen Malone, January 27, 2013

People see celebrities, and they have money and fame. But I'm a human being. I get scared and I get nervous just like everyone else.

Beyoncé, on being human.

As seen in *The Hollywood Reporter*, Sophie Schillaci, January 14, 2013

Power's not given to you. You have to take it.

Beyoncé, on power.

As seen in *The New Republic*, by Noreen Malone,
January 27, 2013

The world will see you the way you see you and treat you the way you treat yourself.

Beyoncé, on self-health.

As seen in *Vanity Fair*, by Julie Miller, April 4, 2016

Having the power to make every final decision and being accountable for them is definitely a burden and a blessing. To me, power is making things happen without asking for permission. It's affecting the way people perceive themselves and the world around them. It's making people stand up with pride.

Beyoncé, on power.

As seen in *Elle*, by Tamar Gottesman, April 4, 2016

Time is the most valuable asset
you own, and you have to use it
wisely. My parents taught me how
to work hard and smart. Both were
entrepreneurs; I watched them
struggle working 18-hour days.
They taught me that nothing worth
having comes easily.

Beyoncé, on time.

As seen in *Elle*, by Tamar Gottesman, April 4, 2016

My father stressed discipline and was tough with me. He pushed me to be a leader and an independent thinker. My mother loved me unconditionally, so I felt safe enough to dream.

Beyoncé, on her father, Mathew Knowles.

As seen in *Elle*, by Tamar Gottesman, April 4, 2016

I learned the importance of honoring my word and commitments from my mother. One of the best things about her is her ability to sense when I am going through a tough time. She texts me the most powerful prayers, and they always come right when I need them. I know I'm tapped into her emotional Wi-Fi.

Beyoncé, on her mother, Tina Knowles.

As seen in *Elle*, by Tamar Gottesman, April 4, 2016

A feminist is someone who believes in equal rights for men and women. I don't understand the negative connotation of the word, or why it should exclude the opposite sex. If you are a man who believes your daughter should have the same opportunities and rights as your son, then you're a feminist.

Beyoncé, on feminism.

As seen in *The Independent*, by Olivia Blair, April 5, 2016

We need men and women to understand the double standards that still exist in this world, and we need to have a real conversation so we can begin to make changes. Ask anyone, man or woman, 'Do you want your daughter to have 75 cents when she deserves $1?' What do you think the answer would be?

Beyoncé, on feminism.

As seen in *The Independent*, by Olivia Blair, April 5, 2016

I hope I can create art that helps
people heal. Art that makes
people feel proud of their struggle.
Everyone experiences pain, but
sometimes you need to be
uncomfortable to transform.
Pain is not pretty, but I wasn't able
to hold my daughter in my arms
until I experienced the pain of
childbirth!

Beyoncé, on art.

As seen in *Elle*, by Tamar Gottesman, April 4, 2016

Don't focus on the aesthetic.
It's really about who you are,
and the human being, that makes
you beautiful.

Beyoncé, on beauty.

As seen in *Elle*, by Natasha Bird, March 31, 2016

I'm not at all shy about having the freedom to wear something fashionable, or something sexy, or showing more skin. I have no problem with being whatever character I need to be. I have my limits, clearly, but I think that's the beauty of being a woman. We have so many different personalities and I love to tap into all of those.

Beyoncé, on freedom.

As seen on *dazeddigital.com*, by Tim Noakes, July 12, 2011

I think it's interesting because people think I'm a lot curvier than I am. I'm definitely not like what people's perception of me is. Every single day of my life somebody says, 'You're tiny!' Every day! I guess everyone else puts more focus on it than I do.

Beyoncé, on public perception.

As seen on *dazeddigital.com*, by Tim Noakes, July 12, 2011

I would love people to stage-dive at my shows. It would be great. I mean, I say that, although if it happens at Glastonbury I'll probably be like, 'Oh, um, wait a minute!'

Beyoncé, on headlining Glastonbury Festival.

As seen on *dazeddigital.com*, by Tim Noakes, July 12, 2011

I would have never thought about doing Glastonbury if I wasn't there the night that Jay-Z played [in 2008]. I guess it's different with pop music as these songs are played at graduations and weddings. **"**

Beyoncé, on headlining Glastonbury Festival.

As seen on *dazeddigital.com*, by Tim Noakes, July 12, 2011

I didn't even know I've had negative press in the past three months! I didn't. I think that's one of the great things about living my life with my family and my friends and the people that I respect and I love. I kind of stand away from that madness. There's always something negative about every celebrity if you're looking for it.

Beyoncé, on press and celebrity.

As seen on *dazeddigital.com*, by Tim Noakes, July 12, 2011

I don't want to hear about why 'Single Ladies' or 'Crazy In Love' were so successful. I don't want to hear it. I believe that there are certain things that happen and they happen naturally.

Beyoncé, on her hits.

As seen on *dazeddigital.com*, by Tim Noakes, July 12, 2011

Being private controls your brand. It controls what you want to put out there and kind of forces people to talk about what you want them to talk about. **99**

Beyoncé, on her brand.

As seen on *mtv.com*, by Jennifer Vineyard, August 10, 2008

66

My father had to fight those battles with racism. I didn't. And now I'm large enough—I'm universal—that no one's paying attention to what race I am. I've kind of proven myself. I'm past that.

99

Beyoncé, on racism.

As seen in *Vogue*, by Jonathan Van Meter, April 1, 2009

Michelle Obama told me she was very happy that her girls have someone like me to look up to … And I'm like, 'Oh, my God.'

Beyoncé, on being a role model.

As seen in *Vogue*, by Jonathan Van Meter, April 1, 2009

I wish there really was a Sasha
Fierce, because I'd send her on
the road and I would go and
do the movies.

Beyoncé, on her alter-ego, Sasha Fierce.

As seen in *Vogue*, by Jonathan Van Meter, April 1, 2009

I definitely make time for my life, it's the most important thing. The music and all that is very important, but I have to have inspiration. 🙸

Beyoncé, on inspiration.

As seen in *Vogue*, by Jonathan Van Meter, April 1, 2009

I'm an ambitious woman, and when I do anything, I do it really hard. If I work out, I work out really hard, if I love somebody, I love them all the way. I'm very loyal. I want a whole bunch of kids—but after I've got certain things out of my system first.

Beyoncé, on ambition.

As seen in *Vogue*, by Jonathan Van Meter, April 1, 2009

When I'm being bad, I'm really bad! I'm talking cheeseburgers, pizzas, French fries . . . You know I'm bad.

Beyoncé, on comfort food.

As seen in the *Mirror*, May 17, 2009

The reality is: Sometimes you lose.
And you're never too good to lose.
You're never too big to lose.
You're never too smart to lose.
It happens.

Beyoncé, on losing.

As seen on *eonline.com*, by Bruna Nessif,
December 18, 2013

If you've been doing all you can and it's not happening for you, go out and have you a good old time . . . move on.

Beyoncé, on dreams.

As seen in *Elle*, by Natasha Bird, March 31, 2016

I'm learning how to drown out the constant noise that is such an inseparable part of my life. I don't have to prove anything to anyone, I only have to follow my heart and concentrate on what I want to say to the world. I run my world. 99

Beyoncé, on who's the boss.

As seen in *Marie Claire*, by Francesca Rice, September 1, 2014

FIVE

RUN THE WORLD

One day in the near future, after she has accomplished even more than she already has, Beyoncé will ditch her famous mononym and change her name one final time: Madam President.

It's inevitable. This is why . . .

We have to teach our boys the rules of equality and respect, so that as they grow up gender equality becomes a natural way of life. And we have to teach our girls that they can reach as high as humanly possible.

Beyoncé, on teaching children.

As seen in *Marie Claire*, by Francesca Rice, September 1, 2014

Being a mother just gives you purpose. I realized why I was born and more than anything all of the things I want to pass onto my child, and the best way of doing that is not by preaching or telling her but showing her by example.

Beyoncé, on motherhood.

As seen in *People*, by Melody Chiu, July 14, 2017

I felt like when I was having contractions, I envisioned my child pushing through a very heavy door. And I imagined this tiny infant doing all the work, so I couldn't think about my own pain ... We were talking. I know it sounds crazy, but I felt a ... *communication.*

Beyoncé, on giving birth.

As seen in *Vogue*, by Jason Gay, February 10, 2013

I'm a workaholic and I don't believe in 'No.' If I'm not sleeping, nobody's sleeping.

Beyoncé, on her work ethic.

As seen in the *Metro*, by Mary Olivia Hickey, September 5, 2016

Your self-worth is determined
by you. You don't have to depend
on someone telling you who
you are.

Beyoncé, on self-worth.

As seen in *Marie Claire*, by Francesca Rice,
September 1, 2014

When I'm not feeling my best,
I ask myself, 'What are you gonna
do about it?' I use the negativity
to fuel the transformation into
a better me.

Beyoncé, on negativity.

As seen in *Time*, Jessie Van Amburg, September 2, 2016

A true diva is graceful, and talented, and strong, and fearless, and brave, and someone with humility.

Beyoncé, on being labelled a diva.

As seen in *Elle*, by Natasha Bird, March 31, 2016

We all have our imperfections.
But I'm human, and you know, it's
important to concentrate on other
qualities besides outer beauty.

Beyoncé, on imperfections.

As seen in *Elle*, by Natasha Bird, March 31, 2016

“

We need to reshape our own perception of how we view ourselves. We have to step up as women and take the lead.

”

Beyoncé, on equality.

As seen in *The Huffington Post*, by Sophie Gallagher, February 9, 2016

I think the most stressful thing for me is balancing work and life. Making sure I am present for my kids—dropping Blue off at school, taking Rumi and Sir to their activities, making time for date nights with my husband, and being home in time to have dinner with my family—all while running a company can be challenging.

Beyoncé, on work-life balance.

As seen in *Elle*, Q&A from fans, December 12, 2019

I'm over being a pop star. I don't want to be a hot girl. I want to be iconic.

Beyoncé, on being a pop star.

As seen on *nme.com*, September 4, 2008

I wanted to sell a million records, and I sold a million records. I wanted to go platinum, and I went platinum. I've been working non-stop since I was 15. I don't even know how to chill out.

Beyoncé, on achieving goals.

As seen on *express.co.uk*, January 2, 2009

The old lessons of submissiveness and fragility made us victims. Women are so much more than that. You can be a businesswoman, a mother, an artist, and a feminist —what ever you want to be— and still be a sexual being. It's not mutually exclusive.

Beyoncé on equality.

As seen in *The Huffington Post*, by Sophie Gallagher, February 9, 2016

I just sacrificed . . . *life*. Being able
to walk down the street and being
able to make mistakes and not have
it recorded for ever, being able to
have regular relationships and dates,
just regular, normal things that
people probably don't even think
about. Sometimes it's hard.

Beyoncé on sacrifices.

As seen in *The Guardian*, by Caspar Llewellyn Smith,
November 29, 2009

I never wanted to be famous for my personal life. I wanted to be famous for my music and my talent, and I always wished I could cut it out when I left the stage. And Jay was private before I met him. It was just who we were. Even before we were celebrities.

Beyoncé, on fame.

As seen in *The Guardian*, by Caspar Llewellyn Smith, November 29, 2009

My daughter introduced me to myself. You know, my mother and I are so close, and I always prayed that I would have that type of relationship with my daughter. And she's still a baby, but the connection I had with her when I was giving birth was something that I've never felt before.

Beyoncé, on mothers and daughters.

As seen on *today.com*, by Danielle Brennan, February 3, 2017

If you don't take the time to think
about and analyze your life, you'll
never realize all the dots that
are all connected.

Beyoncé, on ambition.

As seen on *inc.com*, by Peter Economy, June 4, 2019

Don't try to lessen yourself
for the world; let the world
catch up to you.

Beyoncé, on ambition.

As seen on *inc.com*, by Peter Economy, June 4, 2019

There are many shades on every journey. Nothing is black or white. I've been through hell and back, and I'm grateful for every scar.

Beyoncé, on her journey.

As seen in *Vogue*, by Beyoncé, August 6, 2018